Real Estate Accounting and Taxation

Real Estate Accounting and Taxation

by
John F. Mahoney, CPA

University Readers™
San Diego, CA

First published in the United States of America in 2008 by University Readers

Cover design by Monica Hui Hekman

12 11 10 09 08   1 2 3 4 5

Printed in the United States of America

ISBN: 978-1-934269-26-8 (paper)

University Readers™
800.200.3908 | www.universityreaders.com

Contents

Chapter
One

Choosing Type
of Entity

Choosing Type
of Entity

T here are various forms of ownership that an individual or organization can choose to hold property in. The following is a brief summary of some of them:

SOLE PROPRIETORSHIP:

One individual owns the business. He or she should file a Business Certificate form at the local county court for an *assumed* name, which is also called a "doing business as" certificate (D/B/A.) This filing should help protect the business name.

Advantages of being a sole proprietorship:

1. It's simple to form. Other than filing the Business Certificate referred to above, no other forms are required.

2. It's easy to report and file tax returns for the business. The business itself does not file returns with the government. Instead, the

individual records the income or loss of the business on his or her individual income tax return (Form 1040: Schedule E, page 2, for real estate rentals – which are not subject to self-employment tax - and Schedule C for other business income, including dealer income or loss which is discussed later which is subject to self-employment tax.) This avoidance of tax for the business standing by itself is called a "flow-through", "pass-through" or "conduit". In other words, the business itself doesn't pay or file tax returns, you, the owner must report the income or loss of the business on your individual personal tax return. Pass-through losses are subject to basis limitations and passive – non-passive activities rules, which will be discussed later.

Disadvantages of being a sole proprietorship:

1. Unlimited liability. In addition to loosing your initial investment and any additional accretion to your investment, the owner can be held personally liable for all of the company's debts. For example, you invest $30,000 in your Sole Proprietorship. At the end of the year, you have no assets (including cash) available and debts of $200,000. Your business creditors can hold you personally liable for what is due them. In other words, not only did you loose your initial investment of $30,000, but you may end up paying an additional $200,000 from your personal assets or having leans and/or garnishments filed against you personally for the debts of the business. At this point bankruptcy protection should be contemplated.

2. Additional taxation. As noted above, *except for rentals* (Schedule E filers), the owner is subject to self-employment tax. The following is an example of this additional tax:

Revenues	$	100,000
Less: Expenses		(40,000)
Taxable Income (Net Profit for Self-employment)	$	60,000
@ Self-employment rate		* 92.35%
Income subject to Self-employment Tax	$	55,410
Self-employment Tax Rate		15.30%
Self-employment Tax	$	8,478

* This rate is used to give the self-employed taxpayer a rate reduction equal to the amount of FICA and Medicare Taxes that would have been withheld from their wages had he or she been an employee.

In the example above, the Self-employment Tax is in addition to the Personal Income Tax on the business's income. Assuming all the income is subject to Personal Income Tax (Itemized or Standard Deductions are already factored in), the following is an example of this individual's total tax for the year:

Taxable Income (per above calculation)	$	60,000	
Deduction for one-half of Self-employment Tax		** 4,239	
Taxable Income subject to Personal Income Tax	$	55,761	
Personal Income Tax Rate (Federal only)		35.00%	Rate Varies
Personal Income Tax	$	19,516	from 10 to 35%
Add: Self-employment Tax (Calculated previously)		8,478	
Total Federal Taxes	$	27,994	

** Congress wanted to give some tax relief to sole proprietors and therefore authorized this deduction.

Please note that the 15.3% Self-employment Tax consists of two taxes: a FICA Tax of 12.4% and a Medicare Tax of 2.9%. It is generally twice what an employee pays since the employer is required to match the employee amounts dollar for dollar. Also note that there is a cap on the FICA Tax. For 2005 it was $90,000. There is no cap on the Medicare Tax.

3. Capital infusion is limited to one person, the owner. If the company needs money, the individual owner or some outside lending facility must contribute. If it were a partnership, for example, multiple owners would be able to contribute. This way some of the financial burden could be reduced or spread over more people or entities.

4. Ownership responsibility and creativity rests with one person. It's rare, but not impossible, that the owner has all the qualities needed to run a successful business. These traits include marketing, managing and administering a business. This is one reason why companies have multiple owners. One owner, for example, is great at vendor negotiations, while another owner is good at inspiring employees to be creative, etc.

PARTNERSHIP:

This is when more than one individual combines resources. It is sometimes considered as a merging of two or more sole proprietors for greater utilization of economies of scale, capital inflows, creativity, and enhanced administrative skills.

Similar to a Sole Proprietorship, the partnership is also a conduit, but files an information return with the IRS (Form 1065) in which it details income and expenses of the partnership and notifies the IRS and the individual partners of their respective portions of income or loss and capital basis. This allocation is accomplished using 1065 K-1 forms, which are attached to the partnership information return and also sent to the individual partners. Partners then use this information on their K-1 to report their share of income or loss on their individual income tax return using Schedule E, page 2, (Form 1040.)

Most partnerships should have a "partnership agreement" to protect individual partners. This agreement is a legal document signed by all partners usually detailing continuity in case of death of a partner, etc. This way the partnership can continue even if a partner dies. Generally, if there were no partnership agreement, the partnership would cease upon the death of a partner. The partnership agreement can be modified at any time to include disproportionate allocations of income or loss. (A disproportionate share of income or loss would occur if, for example, you have a 20% share of the partnership but are allowed to have a 60% share of any partnership losses.) The IRS will generally accept disproportionate allocations provided they make economic sense.

The partnership must have at least one General Partner that can be held personally liable for the businesses debts and actions. General Partners actively participate in the affairs of the partnership. For liability purposes they are treated similarly to a Sole Proprietor. But the partnership may form a Limited Partnership in which there must be at least one general partner and all other owners may be deemed Limited Partners and can not be held personally liable for the debts of the business. The state normally requires a list of who is a Limited and who is a General Partner. To qualify as a Limited Partner, you cannot do any managerial work for the business. In other words, you have to be a passive investor to qualify. If you actively participate in the management of the business, you can loose this protection and can be held legally liable for the debts of the business in excess of your investment.

CORPORATION:

This is when one or more individuals or entities purchase common capital stock in the business. These stockholders own the corporation. They usually vote for a Board of Directors who manages the affairs of the corporation by choosing and delegating authority to officers of the corporation.

The ownership is in shares of stock that are offered by the corporation. Corporations can also issue preferred non-voting stock (preference as to dividends and liquidations) but must issue common stock, which is the voting stock referred to above.

The stock can be of a par value or no-par value. Par value has the par value in dollars printed on the face of the stock certificate, and has it listed in the corporation's charter. No par stock has no dollar value printed on the face of the certificate. Both par value and no par value stock are the legal capital, which cannot be withdrawn by stockholders except in liquidation. (Concerning only the par value stock, in case of liquidation, stockholders who bought the stock below par value are liable for the corps debts to the extent of the discount.)

Advantages of being a corporation:

1. Limited liability. Unlike Sole Proprietors or General Partners who can be held personally liable for the debts of the firm, stockholders can "walk away" from liability provided there was no illegal conveyances of assets.

2. Ease of raising capital. Corporations, especially publicly traded corporations, can generally raise capital quickly by issuance of additional common or preferred stock. It does erode the stock value for present common shareholders but they are usually given a "rights" offer allowing them to keep parity with their stock.

3. Ease of transferring ownership rights. A Sole Proprietorship or Partnership sale generally requires an extensive amount of legal work whereas the sale of shares in a Corp. are extremely easy to consummate on the open or private market.

4. Continuous existence. Corporations are stand-alone entities and therefore continuity is assumed. If a shareholder dies, for example, the Corp. doesn't cease. Instead, the estate or beneficiaries receive the shares of the deceased and the Corp. continues with new ownership.

<u>Disadvantages of being a corporation</u>:

1. Additional taxation. Sometimes referred to as "double taxation", the Corporation pays tax on its taxable income and any dividend the Corp. pays to its shareholders is subject to personal income tax for the recipient. In other words, roughly the same income is taxed two times; once at the corporate level and again at the personal level. The only recent benefit is the dividends usually qualify for the lower Capital Gains tax rate (usually 15%).

   One way to avoid this additional taxation is electing IRC Subchapter S (Sub S) status. If all shareholders elect Sub S status, the Corp. doesn't pay tax, but instead, individual shareholders report their proportionate share of income or loss on their respective individual income tax returns. Sub S's have a number of limitations and restrictions. A Sub S cannot have more than 100 shareholders. It cannot have shareholders who are non-resident aliens. Other Corporations or Partnerships cannot be shareholders. Finally, the Sub S election must be unanimous. Please note that earnings from a Sub S are not subject to Self-employment tax but a portion of the Sub S's income may be considered wages and not earnings. In other words, assume that the S Corp. has only one shareholder and that shareholder works entirely for the Corp. That shareholder should pay himself or herself a reasonable salary, subject to FICA & Medicare. If this is not done, the IRS can choose a reasonable salary and charge the S Corp. the applicable FICA & Medicare Taxes. The IRS generally uses Robert Half's Account Temp rates, which are usually much higher because their margin is included in their rates.

2. Accumulated earnings tax. This situation occurs when a Corporation retains excessive amount of earnings instead of paying out these earnings to its shareholders. The Corp. does this to avoid double taxation. Under certain circumstances the IRS may deem a dividend and tax the Corp at the highest personal rate (currently 35%), or at the highest personal capital gains rate (currently 15%). The IRS concentrates on excess liquidity in their calculation of what is excessive. Reasonable business needs may justify the ex-

cess liquidity and accumulation of income and therefore eliminate the tax. These business needs include: business expansion and plant replacement, debt retirement, and maintaining adequate working capital. Besides these amounts, a credit of $250,000 ($150,000 for personal service corporations) is also allowed in the calculation.

3. Limitations on Capital Loss deductions. Capital losses can only offset capital gains. Any excess losses are carried back three years and forward five years to offset capital gains.

REAL ESTATE INVESTMENT TRUST (REIT):

A REIT is a corporation or trust that specializes in investments that are in realty including residential and commercial properties. REITs usually fall into two categories, those that own real estate (Equity REITs) and those that invest in mortgages (Mortgage REITs). (Recent legislation allows REITs to venture into areas that are not solely real estate.) REITs must distribute 90% of their annual net income attributable to real estate to their shareholders. This limits the REITs ability to retain earnings for future acquisitions, etc. These dividends do not qualify for the lower Capital Gains tax rate and therefore, the shareholder recipient is taxed at their higher personal income tax rate.

LIMITED LIABILITY COMPANY (LLC):

An LLC is a company that can be taxed as Sole Proprietorship, Partnership or Corporation. Instead of being called sole proprietors, partners or shareholders, the owners are called members. An LLC is considered as a "disregarded entity" for federal income tax reporting and therefore can be taxed as a Corporation, Partnership or Sole Proprietorship, based on its own choosing. Many LLC's elect to be treated as Partnerships because they can utilize the "Flow-through" of income or loss to individual tax returns of their members. Choosing Partnership treatment also can benefit members to utilize the nonproportionate distribution of income or loss as described in the Partnership section above. If there is only one member and no election is made or checked off, it is assumed that the entity is Sole Proprietorship as opposed to a Corporation and falls under those Sole Proprietorship rules described above. The major differences between an LLC and other entities are: an LLC can have one owner and qualify; an LLC need not have general partners; members can make managerial decisions and not be held personally liable for more than their investment; an LLC can have Corporations, Partnerships, other LLC's, and non-resident aliens as members.

Chapter Two

Key Principles of Real Estate Investing

Key Principles of Real Estate Investing

~~~~~~~~

Investors in real estate ventures generally evaluate their investment similarly to other types of investments. For example both real estate and non real estate investors weigh risk versus return when making a decision to invest or not to invest in something. The following are some principles of investing that pertain more so to the real estate industry than to any other industry.

1. <u>**LEVERAGING (ESPECIALLY NON-RECOURSE)**</u>:

In the real estate industry leveraging is also referred to as using "other peoples money"(OPM). Leveraging is successful if the cost of the borrowed funds is less than the earnings of what those borrowed funds produce. In other words, if more can be earned on the borrowed funds than is paid for the use of them, then the arrangement would be a successful one. Leveraging is also used by owners to diversify risk, assuming the debt is non-recourse.

2. **FLOW-THROUGH TAX BENEFITS**:

    Depreciation is a normal deduction for real estate entities. Many times it will be sufficient enough to produce a loss (not an operating loss but a "paper" loss only.) If this is the case, owners that are partners or sole proprietors may be able to deduct their portion of these losses from their other income with the effect of reducing their individual tax liability. This is assuming the owner has sufficient basis to deduct the loss and that it is a non-passive activity. Both of these areas (basis and passive or non-passive activities) will be discussed later.

3. **SUFFICIENT NON-TAXABLE CASH WITHDRAWALS**:

    This is usually beneficial for Sole Proprietorships, Partnerships and Subchapter S Corps. Part of the owner's return of investment may be in the form of tax-free distributions. These withdrawals would then be considered a return of capital. In other words, if the income has already been taxed to the owners, any distribution up to that amount would generally be considered a tax free or previously tax distribution.

Chapter Three

Basis

Basis

The following excerpts pertain to basis. It should be noted that any mention of "Code" is the Internal Revenue Code (IRC).

BASIS IS USED FOR MANY REASONS:

- It's used to determine the amount of gain or loss the owner(s) have when their business is liquidated or sold.

- It's used to determine if the owner(s) are currently allowed a personal loss deduction on their portion of the businesses losses. (This is discussed in the next section entitled: Loss Deductions.)

CALCULATING BASIS:

Generally, basis in any property depends on how the owner(s) acquired it. There are many ways to acquire property, including:

- **Purchasing the property:**

  This occurs when the owner(s) purchase the real property by paying for it with their own funds or leveraging by paying all or part of the cost via a mortgage. The total costs include the cost of land and any buildings. The cost of land generally stays on the books until liquidation, where as the cost of the buildings are depreciated using a mid-month straight line method whose write-off is 27 ½ years for residential property and 39 years for non-residential property.

- **Constructing the property:**

  This occurs when the owner(s) construct their property. Similar to purchasing the property, the cost is the cost of the land and the additional cost necessary to construct the building or buildings. Incidentally, demolition cost to level a building in order to construct a new building is added to the cost of the land and not the cost of the building.

- **Property acquired by gift:**

  This occurs when the owner(s) are gifted the property. Generally, the basis of the property acquired by gift is the basis the donor had in the property at the time the gift was made.

- **Property acquired by inheritance:**

  This occurs when the property owner dies and the estate transfers the property to the beneficiaries. Generally, under Code Sec. 1041, the basis of the property acquired by inheritance is the "stepped-up" basis, which is the fair market value of the property on the date of the decedent's death. (Starting January 1, 2010, the "stepped-up" basis will be repealed and a modified basis will be substituted with the beneficiary getting a basis in the property of the lower of the adjusted basis of the property in the hands of the decedent or the fair market value of the property on the date of the decedent's death.)

- **Property acquired in a tax-free exchange:**

This occurs when property that an owner has is exchanged with property that another owner has. Generally, in accordance with Code Sec. 1031 (d), gain or loss is not recognized when property held for productive use in a trade or business is exchanged for property of a "like kind". The basis of the old property becomes the basis of the new property. This basis is also called the "substituted basis" and will remain (net of subsequent depreciation) until the asset is disposed of. "Like kind" exchanges will be discussed shortly.

Chapter
Four

Limitations on Loss Deductions

Limitations on Loss Deductions

One of the key principles of real estate investing noted above is the flow-through of tax benefits to the investor. This means that if the business has a loss, individual investors may be able to use their proportional share of the loss to offset their other personal taxable income. But, there are two limitations to the amount of loss that can be used. The first is a "basis" or "at risk" limitation and the second is a "passive" limitation. These limitations are explained as follows:

1. **<u>BASIS LIMITATION</u>:**

    Generally, losses for sole proprietors, partners and subchapter S shareholders are limited to their basis in their investment plus any debt that they personally guaranteed for the entity. In totality, these amounts would be considered "at risk" to the owner. In other words, this is what the owner is actually risking if the business fails. Therefore, for example, the maximum amount of loss that a Sole Proprietor could deduct personally would be his or her initial investment, plus any subsequent additional investments that they made to the company, including property, plus all prior year's earnings, plus all amounts owed by the business, less all prior year's losses, and finally, less any withdrawals (drawings) ever paid or any property ever distributed to themselves. As an example, assume you are a Sole Proprietor and your business has a $125,000 loss in year two. How much of that loss, if any, could you use as a deduction to reduce other income on your personal income tax return?:

Owner's initial capital contribution to the business	$100,000
Taxable Income for Year 1	50,000
"At Risk" Basis at start of Year 2	$150,000

Since the "at risk" basis exceeds the loss in year two, the entire loss of $125,000 could be used as a deduction. In other words, there is sufficient basis to qualify the deduction. Let's now assume that the taxable income in year one was only $10,000. This would mean that the "at risk" was only $110,000 and consequently, only $110,000 could offset other personal income in the current year. The $15,000 unused loss would then be carried over and used in future years as a offset to income. IRS Form 6198 can be used to calculate deductible "at risk" losses and also can be used to report any carryover amount.

For a General Partner, the maximum amount of loss deductible is similar to that of a Sole Proprietor noted above. For a Limited partner, referred to previously, it's the same as a General Partner, except that the amounts owed by the business are not the responsibility of the Limited Partner, in other words they are not "at risk" and consequently, these amounts would not be used in the calculation. The only exception to the "at risk" limitation is qualified nonrecourse financing of real property. If the nonrecourse financing meets the following criteria, it can be considered in the deductible loss calculation:

- The borrowing must be for real estate.

- The lender must be qualified (most lenders qualify).

- The loan cannot involve convertible debt.

For a Subchapter S Shareholder, the loss is similar to a Limited Partner except for the nonrecourse financing which is not allowed in the calculation because corporations are separate entities whose shareholders are entitled to limited liability. This favorable treatment given to unincorporated entities is one of the major reasons why companies holding real estate do not usually choose corporations as their entity. To receive the favorable tax treatment and also have limited liability, they should choose Limited Liability Company (LLC) or Limited Liability Partnership (LLP) and check off Sole Proprietorship or Partnership when applying for an ID# with the IRS (SS 4 Form). The only exception is a Real Estate Investment Trust (REIT) which is generally required to be a Corporation.

2. <u>PASSIVE ACTIVITY LOSS LIMITATION</u>:

In regards to utilizing flow-through benefits, losses from passive activities generally can *only* be used to offset income from passive activities. Passive activities are those where the owner does not materially participate in the business. Passive activities do not include "earned income' activities such as wages or "portfolio income". (Portfolio income includes income earned on interest, dividends, annuities and royalties, as well as gains or losses from the sale of non-trade or business property.) If passive losses cannot be used as a current deduction, any unused losses are then carried over to future years. If the business is liquidated or sold, any unused loss carryover will reduce gains or increase losses on the sale of the business. Rental activities, according to IRS Sec, 469c(1), always default to passive activities unless the owner "actively" participates in the business. The "active" participation is much less stringent than the "material" participation referred to later for real estate professionals. To qualify as an "active" participant, the owner must own at least 10% of the business, make management decisions (for example: approving new tenants or expenditures) in a bona fide sense. Further to the deduction for losses from rental activities, there is an annual $25,000 limit. In other words, the maximum amount of rental passive activity losses that an individual can use to offset nonpassive income is $25,000. The balance of the losses can offset passive income. Any losses still available can be carried over to future years. The annual $25,000 limit is reduced for higher income individuals $.50 for each $1 dollar of adjusted gross income in excess of $100,000 and consequently phased out when the individual's adjusted gross income reaches $150,000.

REAL ESTATE PROFESSIONALS:

Some real estate professionals may be able to treat rental real estate activities as non-passive. They are generally called *dealers*. To qualify as a *dealer*, they must *materially* participate in the business and perform more than 750 hours of service for the business during the year and this constitutes more than half the time performing all services during the year. The 750 hours must be in rental real estate ventures and not commingled with other business ventures. All the income and losses of *dealers* in realty is considered ordinary and therefore not subject to capital gain or loss treatment. The only exception allowed is property held for investment purposes. Finally, *dealers* are not allowed to use the Installment Method to report gains on any property disposed of during the year except residential lots and certain timeshare rights provided the *dealer* held such rights for not more than six weeks per year.

Chapter
Five

Like-Kind Tax-Free Exchanges

Like-Kind Tax-Free Exchanges

G enerally, when business or investment property is sold, gain or loss is recognized immediately for tax purposes. However, under IRS Code Sec. 1031, you can defer some or all of this gain or loss provided certain conditions are met. Utilizing Sec. 1031, no gain or loss is recognized on the exchange of property held for productive use in a trade or business or for investment provided that the property is *exchanged* for property of a *like-kind*. Any unrecognized gain or loss is not eliminated or absolved. Instead, the unrecognized gain or loss on the like-kind exchange is preserved in the basis of the replacement property. Therefore, recognition, if any, is postponed until the property is sold or otherwise disposed of in the future.

For example, suppose you exchange a parcel of land that you purchased for $100,000 a few years ago for a building valued at $140,000. The gain realized would of course be $40,000, calculated as follows:

Market Value of Property Acquired (Building)	$ 140,000
Less: Basis of Old Property (Land)	(100,000)
Gain Realized	$ 40,000

If this transaction qualified as an IRS Code Sec. 1031 exchange, none of this gain would be taxable immediately. Instead, recognition would be postponed by reducing your basis for the new property. In other words, the basis for the new property would be the basis of the property you transferred. In our example above, the basis for your new property would be $100,000 and not the market value of $140,000, calculated as follows:

Market Value of Property Acquired (Building)	$140,000
Less: Gain Realized but not Recognized	(40,000)
Adjusted Basis of New Property (Building)	$100,000

This Adjusted Basis for the new property is sometimes referred to a substituted basis (you are substituting your old basis for the value of the replacement property).

It should be noted that there are no limitations on the number of times you can elect using Sec. 1031 treatment. In the above example, if you exchanged the building that you acquired for some other like-kind property, you could postpone recognition on any gain or loss on the new transaction.

It should also be noted that if you receive money or non like-kind property as part of a like-kind transaction, gain is recognized to the extent of the non like-kind property and or the money received, but a loss will not be recognized.

EXCLUDED PROPERTY:

The following property does not qualify for Sec. 1031 treatment:

1. Real Property exchanged for Personal Property.

2. Inventory or any property held primarily for sale, including real estate held by dealers.

3. Property used for personal purposes, including homes, autos, furniture, etc.

4. Stocks, bonds, notes or any other holdings of indebtedness such as accounts receivable.

5. Partnership interests.

6. Certificates of trust or beneficial interests.

7. Property located outside the United States.

8. Choses in action.

WHAT QUALIFIES AS "LIKE-KIND" PROPERTY?:

Like-kind refers more to the *nature* of the property and not the grade or quality of the property. Like-kind properties are properties of the same nature (or character) even if they differ in grade and or quality. If it's real estate property, for example, it doesn't matter if it's improved or unimproved. Therefore, you could exchange land for buildings and qualify for this favorable tax treatment.

An exchange of real estate that you own for a real estate lease that runs 30 years or longer will qualify for a like-kind exchange.

DEFERRED EXCHANGES:

Sec. 1031 requires you to identify the property to be received within 45 days after the date you transferred the property that you gave up in the exchange. The identification must include a signed written document that clearly describes the replacement property and must be sent to the other party involved in the exchange. The replacement property must be received within 180 days after you transferred the original property that you gave up in the exchange.

USE OF QUALIFIED INTERMEDIARIES:

A qualified intermediary is a person who enters into a written exchange agreement with you to acquire and transfer the property you want to give up and to acquire the replacement property and transfer it to you. If you use a Qualified Intermediary, the transfer of the property given up and receipt of the like-kind property is treated as tax deferred exchange.

REPORTING REQUIREMENTS:

Like-kind Exchanges must be reported on IRS Form 8824 in the year that you transferred the property, even if no gain or loss is recognized. Any portion of the gain or loss recognized (because you received money or non like-kind property) would additionally be reported on IRS Schedule D or Form 4797 as applicable.

Chapter
Six

Accounting

Accounting

GENERALLY ACCEPTED ACCOUNTING PRINCIPLES (GAAP):

All accounting, including financial statements, should conform to generally accepted accounting principles (GAAP). GAAP are accounting principles that developed over time. These principles are scrutinized and modified where necessary and mandate the way accounting statements should be presented and how accounting transactions should be recorded. They are sometimes regarded as rules or guidelines. Congress created the Securities and Exchange Commission (SEC) in 1934 which has the authority to regulate GAAP. Even thou the SEC has the responsibility for GAAP, it generally delegates this authority to other bodies. The present body responsible for maintaining GAAP in the United States is the Financial Accounting Standards Board (FASB), which was formed in 1973 and issues Statements on Financial Accounting Standards (FAS) and Interpretations (FIN) that establish GAAP for specific accounting issues. Prior to the FASB, the American Institute of Certified Public Accountants (AICPA) promulgated GAAP utilizing its Accounting Principle Board which issued Opinions (APB) and Accounting Research Bulletins (ARB) detailing their position on specific GAAP.

All financial statements should be presented using GAAP. Some GAAP assumptions are as follows:

- **<u>CONTINUITY</u>:**

  It is assumed that the company is a "going concern". In other words, unless otherwise stated in the financial statements, it is assumed that the company should remain viable for an indefinite period of time. If this is not the case, in other word, if a company's solvency appears to be in jeopardy, the entity must state this in their financial statements (usually in the report page as well as in the notes that accompany the financial statement). The components of financial statements will be discussed in the next section.

- **<u>SEPARATE BUSINESS ENTITY</u>:**

  Commingling of personal and business transactions are not proper. The transactions and financial statements of the entity should be separate from the owners of the entity.

- **<u>HISTORICAL COST</u>:**

  Except for marketable securities, all accounting valuation presentations are based on the lower of Historical Cost or Market. For example, if an asset is worth more today that what you paid for it, the cost (reduced for depreciation, if any) and not the appreciated value would still be reflected on the financial statements. This Historical Cost presentation is generally hotly contested in the real estate industry. Most realty owners want to use Market Value on their Balance Sheets and not the lower of Historical Cost or Market. Because Market Value is usually higher, Balance Sheets are, for example, understated. Incidentally, this is one of the major factors that is holding up acceptance of International or Global GAAP. While we in the United States follow Historical Cost, Europe, for example, uses Market Value in any of their presentations.

- ## CONSERVATISM:

Where there is a choice of measurement, the company should select the measurement that is least favorable to the company's financial statements. An example would be writing off an expense currently that couldn't be matched to any specific time period. Instead of waiting to write off the expense in a subsequent period, the company should choose writing it off right now. An opposite example would be deferring revenue from the current period to a future period when the earnings recognition is not clear.

Some companies may be more or less conservative than other companies. An example would be how companies implemented the Financial Accounting Standard Board's FAS #106 (Accounting for Postretirement Benefits other than Pensions). This FAS generally lowered Net Income in the implementation year. The FAS gave a choice of when to implement the changes. It wanted companies to implement to FAS by 1993, but allowed earlier implementation. Companies that made the changes in 1992 were more conservative than the ones who waited until 1993 to implement the negative charge to income.

- ## ACCRUAL BASIS:

Under the Accrual Method, Revenue is recognized when it is earned and expenses are recognized when they are incurred. This usually presents the companies financial position in a clearer way as opposed to the cash basis. In the cash basis, revenue is recognized when received (regardless of when the revenue was earned) and expenses are recognized when they are paid (regardless of the period for which the expense was incurred). GAAP mandates the Accrual Method. The presenter must justify any diversion from the Accrual Method.

- **CONSISTENCY**:

  For comparative purposes, the company should use the same accounting treatment from period to period.

- **DISCLOSURE**:

  The Company should disclose all-important items that may influence the judgment of an informed reader. For example, if the company changes its accounting treatment of some transactions, this would have to be disclosed because the consistency assumption referred to above would be affected.

FINANCIAL STATEMENTS:

Financial statements are used to evaluate how a company is doing. If they are presented utilizing an outside accountant firm they will include a Report Page in which the accounting firm gives their opinion of the financial statements. There are four types of opinions:

1. **Unqualified Opinion:**

   In this opinion the accounting firm states that the financial statements are presented fairly and are in conformity with GAAP. It's also referred to as a "Clean Report".

2. **Qualified Opinion:**

   In this opinion the accounting firm states that except for certain specified matters, the financial statements are presented fairly and are in conformity with GAAP. An example of an exception that would qualify an opinion would be changing the accounting treatment of certain transactions. For example, assume that the company changed its method of revenue recognition. Let's also assume that the company is justified in doing this. Because the consistency principle is being violated, the accountant would have to qualify the opinion by stating that the company changed is way of recording revenue. The Notes to the Financial Statements will also describe how the company recognizes revenue and how much the current year's income was affected by the change.

3. **Adverse Opinion:**

In this opinion the accounting firm states that the financial statements are not presently fairly in conformity with GAAP. An example would be a company using the cash basis instead of the Accrual Method when presenting their financial statements.

4. **Disclaimer of Opinion:**

In this opinion the accounting firm states that they cannot express an opinion on the financial statements. The major reason would be lack of independence for the accounting firm.

There are three types of reports that can be presented by the accounting firm. These include:

1. **Audited Report:**

This is the highest type of report with the most exposure for the outside accounting firm. The outside accounting firm will usually test the accuracy of the transactions and verify the company's internal control. All publicly traded companies are required to file an annual audited report.

2. **Reviewed Report**:

This report is less than an audit. The outside accounting firm does some analytical work including ratio analysis. Generally speaking, no verification is mandated for a review. All publicly traded companies are required to file three quarterly reports per annum (the 4th quarter is not a requirement of the SEC but is usually presented with the annual audited report).

3. **Compiled Report**:

This report has less professional weight than an audited or a reviewed report. No verification or analytical work is usually done. It's unacceptable for SEC reporting but lending institutions may consider a compilation as part of their decision making process.

There are three major components that comprise a full set of financial statements. They include a balance sheet, income statement, and statement of cash flows. In addition, there should be a statement of retained earnings (if the entity is a Corporation) or statement of owner's equity (for a Partnership) or statement of capital (for a Sole Proprietorship.) Finally, there should be notes to the financial statements which include information that an informed reader is entitled to know that is not included in the prior statements. The following is a brief description of the three major components:

- **BALANCE SHEET**:

The balance sheet presents the financial condition of the company at a certain date, such as December 31. It shows the health of the company. It's comprised of Assets (things that the company owns), Liabilities (things that the company owes), & Equity (things that the owners are entitled to if the company liquidates, subsequent to satisfying all creditors.) The "Basic Accounting Equation" is that the Assets equal the Liabilities and Equity (A = L + E.)

- ## INCOME STATEMENT:

  The income statement enumerates for a period of time the company's operations, such as for the Year Ending December 31. From looking at the income statement a reader can determine if a company is making a profit or not. Generally, revenues minus expenses equal a profit or a loss. The "Extended Basic Accounting Equation" is that the Assets equal Liabilities and Equity Plus Revenues less Expenses (A = L + E + R - E.)

- ## STATEMENT OF CASH FLOWS:

  The statement of cash flows show for a period of time how a company acquired its cash and how it spent it. It categorizes the receipts and disbursements into three activities: cash flows from Operating Activities, cash flows from Investing Activities, and cash flows from Financing Activities. Operating Activities are net cash from the company's operations; Investing Activities are net cash from transactions involving property, plant, equipment; Financing Activities are net cash involving the liability and Equity side of the balance sheet other than Operating Activities (in other words, it does not include accounts payable, wages payable, etc).

The following are examples of the accounting for and presentation of Partnership and Corporation financial statements:

Partnership Accounting
Example

⤞⤝

T he Jones Company was formed as an LLC in early January, 2005. They used the "Check-Off" method to declare that the entity be taxed as a partnership. The partnership agreement specifies that all four owners contribute and share equally in the venture.

The following is a list of transactions that occurred during the month of January, 2005:

01/03/05:

     The four partners contribute $350,000 each for a total capital of $1,400,000.

01/16/05:

     They purchased a new 100 unit commercial building for $6,250,000, including land of $900,000. The purchase price includes all capitalized expenses. The company contributed $1,250,000 and a bank with a 8.50% 15-year self-amortizing non-recourse mortgage financed the balance of $5,000,000. The first payment of interest starts February 1st (for the 15 day period 1/16/05 through 1/31/05. Principal payments start March 1st. Interest is calculated using 365-day year and 29 days for month of February, 2005.

01/16/05:

They deposit $168,181.82 of tenant rent security representing two months rent from all their tenants. All tenant leases commence February 1, 2005 and payments are due on the 15th of the month for the current month.

The following is a summary of all the transactions occurring during the period February 1, 2005 through December 31, 2005:

1. Rentals: For the 11 months ended 12/31/05, the company collected $912,500 and is due $12,500 from tenants for the month of December, 2005.

2. Operating Expenses: For the 11 months ended 12/31/05, the company incurred $350,000 in operating expenses of which it paid $286,00 during the year and the balance during CYE 2006.

3. The company made all of its mortgage payments on the 1st of each month except for January 1, 2006 payment was made December 31, 2005 to accelerate the flow through interest deduction to the partners.

4. Partners withdrew $25,000 each during CYE 2005.

Assumptions:

- Depreciation is calculated using a 39-year straight life and mid-month convention.

- No vacancy or bad debts during CYE 2005.

REQUIRED:

1. Based on the above information, prepare a Balance Sheet, Income Statement, Statement of Owner's Equity, and Statement of Cash Flows for the company for the CYE 2005.

2. What is the flow through amount for each partner's CYE 2005 personal income tax return?

The Jones Company, LLC.

CYE 2005 Transactions

DATE		DEBIT	CREDIT
1/3/2005	Cash	1,400,000	
	Capital		1,400,000
	To record capital inflow.		
1/15/2005	Land & Building	6,250,000	
	Mortgage Payable		5,000,000
	Cash		1,250,000
	To record building purchase.		
1/16/2005	Cash	168,181.82	
	Tenant Security Deposits		168,181.82
	To record receipt of security deposits.		

02/01/05 through 12/31/05:

	DEBIT	CREDIT
Cash	912,500	
Rent Receivable	12,500	
Rental Income		925,000
To record rent earned during CYE 2005.		
Operating Expenses	350,000	
Cash		286,000
Accounts Payable		64,000
To record expenses incurred during CYE 2005.		
Interest Expense - Mortgage	401,948.38	
Mortgage Payable	157,124.15	
Cash		559,072.53
To record interest paid & amortization of mortgage during CYE 2005.		

The Jones Company, LLC. *(Continued)*
CYE 2005 Transactions

DATE		DEBIT	CREDIT
Partner's Drawings Accounts		100,000	
Cash			100,000
To record distributions to partners during CYE 2005.			
Depreciation Expense -		131,663.50	
Accum. Deprec. - Bldg.			131,663.50
To record depreciation expense for CYE 2005			
(6,250,000 - 900,000) @ 2.461%			

1.

The Jones Company, LLC
Income Statement
For the CYE 12/31/05

Rental Income	$ 925,000
Less: Operating Expenses	350,000
Operating Income	$ 575,000
Less: Depreciation Expense	(131,664)
Interest Expense	(401,948)
Net Income for CYE 12/31/2005	$ 41,388

The Jones Company, LLC
Statement of Owner's Equity
For the Year Ended 12/31/05

Capital Contributions	$ 1,400,000
Add: Net Income for CYE 2005	41,388
	$ 1,441,388
Less: Withdrawals by Owners during CYE 2005	(100,000)
Owner's Equity 12/31/2005	$ 1,341,388

The Jones Company, LLC
Balance Sheet
December 31, 2005

Assets:

Current Assets:

Cash		$ 285,609
Tenant Rent Receivables		12,500
Total Current Assets		$ 298,109

Property, Plant & Equipment:

Land	$ 900,000	
Building	5,350,000	
	$ 6,250,000	
Less: Accumulated Depreciation	(131,664)	
Net Property, Plant & Equipment		6,118,336
Total Assets		$ 6,416,445

Liabilities & Owner's Equity:

Current Liabilities:

Accounts Payable		$ 64,000
Mortgage Payable - Current Portion		186,462
Total Current Liabilities		$ 250,462

Long-Term Liabilities:

Mortgage Payable - Net of Current Portion		4,656,413
Tenant Security Deposits		168,182
Total Long-Term Liabilities		4,824,595
Total Liabilities		$ 5,075,057

Owner's Equity		1,341,388
Total Liabilities & Owner's Equity		$ 6,416,445

The Jones Company, LLC

Statement of Cash Flows

For the CYE 12/31/05

Cash Flows From Operating Activities:

Net Income	$ 41,388
Add: Depreciation	131,664
Increase in Tenant Security Deposits	168,182
Increase in Accounts Payable	64,000
Less: Increase in Tenant Rent Receivable	(12,500)
Net Cash Flows Provided By Operating Activities	$ 392,734

Cash Flows From Investing Activities:

Cash Paid for Purchase of Land and Building	$ (1,250,000)
Net Cash Flows Used For Investing Activities	$ (1,250,000)

Cash Flows From Financing Activities:

Capital Contributions by Owners	$ 1,400,000
Paydown of Mortgage During Year	(157,125)
Payments Made to Owners During Year	(100,000)
Net Cash Flows Provided By Financing Activities	$ 1,142,875

Increase in Cash During Year	$ 285,609

2. **The Flow Through amount on each partner's personal income tax return for CYE 2005 is $10,347. This amount is calculated @ 25% of the Net Income for the year of $41,288.**

REIT Accounting Example

T he Smith Company was formed as an REIT in early January, 2005. In order to conserve earnings, the corporation has decided to pay out the minimum amount of dividends specified annually to maintain its REIT status.

The following is a list of transactions that occurred during the month of January, 2005:

01/03/05:

> The Corporation issued 25,000 shares of $1.00 Par Value for a total of $1,400,000.

01/16/05:

> The Corporation purchased a new 100 unit commercial building for $6,250,000, including land of $900,000. The purchase price includes all capitalized expenses. The company contributed $1,250,000 and the balance of $5,000,000 was financed by a bank with a 8.50% 15 year self-amortizing mortgage. The first payment of interest

starts February 1st (for the 15 day period 1/16/05 through 1/31/05. Principal payments start March 1st. Interest is calculated using 365 day year and 29 days for month of February, 2005.

01/16/05:

The Corporation deposited $168,181.82 of tenant rent security representing two months rent from all their tenants. Per the lease agreements, rents for all tenants are scheduled to increase 5% starting January, 2006. All tenant leases commenced February 1, 2005 and payments are due on the 15th of the month for the current month.

The following is a summary of all the transactions occurring during the period February 1, 2005 through December 31, 2005:

1. Rentals: For the 11 months ended 12/31/05, the company collected $912,500 and is due $12,500 from tenants for the month of December, 2005.

2. Operating Expenses: For the 11 months ended 12/31/05, the company incurred $350,000 in operating expenses of which it paid $286,00 during the year and the balance during CYE 2006.

3. The company made all of its mortgage payments on the 1st of each month except for the January 1, 2006 payment made on December 31, 2005.

4. As noted above, the corporation declared and paid all its required dividends during the year.

The following is a summary of all the transactions occurring during the period January 1, 2006 through December 31, 2006:

1. Rentals: For the 12 months ended 12/31/06, tenants were billed $1,059,545 in monthly rentals. The company collected $1,006,568 during CYE 2006 and the balance of $52,977 in January, 2007. The company also collected 100% of its 12/31/05 tenant receivables during the month of January, 2006.

2. Operating Expenses: For the CYE 2006, the company incurred $391,361 in operating expenses of which it paid $313,090 during the year and the balance during CYE 2007.

3. The company made all of its mortgage payments on the 1st of each month except for the January 1, 2007 payment made on December 31, 2006.

4. Again, as noted above, the corporation declared and paid all its required dividends during the year.

Assumptions:

- Depreciation is calculated using a 39 year straight life and mid-month convention.
- No vacancy or bad debts during CYE 2005 and 2006.

<u>REQUIRED:</u>

1. Based on the above information, prepare a Balance Sheet, Income Statement, Statement of Retained Earnings, and Statement of Cash Flows for the company for the CYE 2005 and 2006

		DEBIT	CREDIT

The Smith Company, Inc.
CYE 2005 Transactions

DATE		DEBIT	CREDIT
1/3/2005	Cash	1,400,000	
	Capital Stock - Common		25,000
	Paid-In-Capital - Common Stock		1,375,000
	To record cash inflow.		
1/15/2005	Land & Building	6,250,000	
	Mortgage Payable		5,000,000
	Cash		1,250,000
	To record building purchase.		
1/16/2005	Cash	168,181.82	
	Tenant Security Deposits		168,181.82
	To record receipt of security deposits.		

02/01/05 through 12/31/05:

DATE		DEBIT	CREDIT
	Cash	912,500	
	Rent Receivable	12,500	
	Rental Income		925,000
	To record rent earned during CYE 2005.		
	Operating Expenses	350,000	
	Cash		286,000
	Accounts Payable		64,000
	To record expenses incurred during CYE 2005.		
	Interest Expense - Mortgage	401,948.38	
	Mortgage Payable	157,124.15	
	Cash		559,072.53
	To record interest paid & amortization of mortgage during CYE 2005.		
	Depreciation Expense - Building	131,663.50	
	Accum. Deprec. - Bldg.		131,663.50
	To record depreciation expense for CYE 2005		
	(6,250,000 - 900,000) @ 2.461%		
	Retained Earnings	39,318.60	
	Cash		39,318.60
	To record dividends paid during CYE 2005 @ 95% of $41,388		

The Smith Company, Inc.
CYE 2006 Transactions

	DEBIT	CREDIT
Cash	12,500	
Rent Receivable		12,500

To record receipt of CYE 2005 balance due.

	DEBIT	CREDIT
Cash	1,006,568	
Rent Receivable	52,977	
Rental Income		1,059,545

To record rent earned during CYE 2006.

	DEBIT	CREDIT
Accounts Payable	64,000	
Cash		64,000

To record payments made during CYE 2006 for CYE 2005 Expenses.

	DEBIT	CREDIT
Operating Expenses	391,361	
Cash		313,090
Accounts Payable		78,271

To record expenses incurred during CYE 2006.

	DEBIT	CREDIT
Interest Expense - Mortgage	404,378.10	
Mortgage Payable	186,462.46	
Cash		590,843.76

To record interest paid & amortization of mortgage during CYE 2006.

The Smith Company, Inc. *(Continued)*

CYE 2006 Transactions

	DEBIT	CREDIT
Depreciation Expense - Building	137,174	
Accum. Deprec. Bldg.		137,174
To record depreciation expense for CYE 2006		
(6,250,000 - 900,000) @ 2.564%		
Retained Earnings	113,968.80	
Cash		113,968.80
To record dividends paid during CYE 2006 @ 90% of $126,632		

The Smith Company, Inc.
Income Statement
For the CYE 12/31/05

Rental Income	$	925,000
Less: Operating Expenses		350,000
Operating Income	$	575,000
Less: Depreciation Expense		(131,664)
Interest Expense		(401,948)
Net Income for CYE 12/31/2005	$	41,388

The Smith Company, Inc.
Statement of Retained Earnings
For the Year Ended 12/31/05

Retained Earnings 01/01/05	$	-
Add: Net Income for CYE 2005		41,388
	$	41,388
Less: Dividends declared and paid during CYE 2005		(39,319)
Retained Earnings 12/31/05	$	2,069

The Smith Company,
Balance Sheet
December 31, 2005

Assets:		
Current Assets:		
Cash	$	346,290
Tenant Rent Receivables		12,500
Total Current Assets	$	358,790

The Smith Company, *(Continued)*
Balance Sheet
December 31, 2005

Property, Plant & Equipment:

Land	$ 900,000	
Building	5,350,000	
	$ 6,250,000	
Less: Accumulated Depreciation	(131,664)	
Net Property, Plant & Equipment		6,118,336
Total Assets		**$ 6,477,126**

Liabilities & Shareholder's Equity:

Current Liabilities:

Accounts Payable	$ 64,000
Mortgage Payable - Current Portion	186,462
Total Current Liabilities	$ 250,462

Long-Term Liabilities:

Mortgage Payable - Net of Current Portion	4,656,413
Tenant Security Deposits	168,182
Total Long-Term Liabilities	4,824,595
Total Liabilities	**$ 5,075,057**

Shareholder's Equity:

Capital Stock - Common, Issued and outstanding, 25,000 Shares, $1 Par Value	$ 25,000
Paid in Capital in Excess of Par Value	1,375,000
Total Capital Stock	$ 1,400,000
Retained Earnings	2,069
Total Shareholder's Equity	$ 1,402,069
Total Liabilities and Shareholder's Equity	$ 6,477,126

The Smith Company, Inc.

Statement of Cash Flows

For the CYE 12/31/05

Cash Flows From Operating Activities:

Net Income	$ 41,388
Add: Depreciation	131,664
Increase in Tenant Security Deposits	168,182
Increase in Accounts Payable	64,000
Less: Increase in Tenant Rent Receivable	(12,500)
Net Cash Flows Provided By Operating Activities	$ 392,734

Cash Flows From Investing Activities:

Cash Paid for Purchase of Land and Building	$ (1,250,000)
Net Cash Flows Used For Investing Activities	$ (1,250,000)

Cash Flows From Financing Activities:

Issuance of Common Stock	$ 1,400,000
Paydown of Mortgage During Year	(157,125)
Dividends Paid	(39,319)
Net Cash Flows Provided By Financing Activities	$ 1,203,556
Increase in Cash During Year	$ 346,290

The Smith Company, Inc.
Income Statement
For the CYE 12/31/06

Rental Income	$ 1,059,545
Less: Operating Expenses	391,361
Operating Income	$ 668,184
Less: Depreciation Expense	(137,174)
Interest Expense	(404,378)
Net Income for CYE 12/31/2006	$ 126,632

The Smith Company, Inc.
Statement of Retained Earnings
For the Year Ended 12/31/06

Retained Earnings 01/01/06	$ 2,069
Add: Net Income for CYE 2006	126,632
	$ 128,701
Less: Dividends declared and paid during CYE 2006	(113,969)
Retained Earnings 12/31/06	$ 14,732

The Smith Company, Inc.
Balance Sheet
December 31, 2006

Assets:

Current Assets:

Cash		$ 283,455
Tenant Rent Receivables		52,977
Total Current Assets		$ 336,432

Property, Plant & Equipment:

Land	$	900,000
Building		5,350,000
	$	6,250,000
Less: Accumulated Depreciation		(268,837)
Net Property, Plant & Equipment		5,981,163
Total Assets		**$ 6,317,595**

The Smith Company, *(Continued)*
Inc.
Balance Sheet

December 31, 2006

Liabilities & Shareholder's Equity:

Current Liabilities:

Accounts Payable	$ 78,268
Mortgage Payable - Current Portion	202,830
Total Current Liabilities	$ 281,098

Long-Term Liabilities:

Mortgage Payable - Net of Current Portion	4,453,583
Tenant Security Deposits	168,182
Total Long-Term Liabilities	4,621,765
Total Liabilities	$ 4,902,863

Shareholder's Equity:

Capital Stock - Common, Issued and outstanding, 25,000 Shares, $1 Par Value	$ 25,000
Paid in Capital in Excess of Par Value	1,375,000
Total Capital Stock	$ 1,400,000
Retained Earnings	14,732
Total Shareholder's Equity	$ 1,414,732
Total Liabilities and Shareholder's Equity	$ 6,317,595

The Smith Company, Inc.

Statement of Cash Flows

For the CYE 12/31/06

Cash Flows From Operating Activities:

Net Income	$ 126,632
Add: Depreciation	137,174
Increase in Accounts Payable	14,271
Less: Increase in Tenant Rent Receivable	(40,477)
Net Cash Flows Provided By Operating Activities	$ 237,600

Cash Flows From Investing Activities:

	$ -
	$ -

Cash Flows From Financing Activities:

Paydown of Mortgage During Year	$ (186,466)
Dividends Paid	(113,969)
Net Cash Flows Provided By Financing Activities	$ (300,435)
(Decrease) in Cash During Year	$ (62,835)
Cash Beginning of Year	346,290
Cash 12/31/06	$ 283,455

Chapter
Seven

Utilizing Ratio Analysis
for Decision Making

Utilizing Ratio Analysis
for Decision Making

M ost efficient businesses use ratio analysis to determine how their company is doing as a standalone and as compared to other companies in their industry. The analysis can be used by internal managers to facilitate strategic decision making and can also be used by investors and lenders to gauge the company's growth potential and credit worthiness. These ratios are percentages that, unlike absolute dollars, level the playing field and are much more useful when making comparisons for the same company or with other companies in the same industry. Only using absolute dollars will severely cripple any analytical observations.

There are two methods that most analysts use to calculate ratios. They are called vertical and horizontal common size analysis. Vertical ratios are calculated by dividing each number on a statement in a particular year into the largest figure on that statement. For example, in a REIT, rental income would be the largest figure on the income statement and consequently, its percentage will be 100. Therefore, all the other income and expense figures would be divided into rental income to arrive at their percentage which in essence is their individual relationship to the largest figure. Vertical common size analysis are standalone ratios in which each year is calculated without regard for any other year and then each year's percentages are compared to each other. Horizontal ratios, on the other hand, are calculated by dividing all figures for all years into a base year set of figures which usually are the earliest figures presented. In other words, horizontal ratios show the increase or decrease between years while vertical ratios show each year's ratios independent of other years and these can be compared to those other years.

The following is an example of vertical and horizontal common size analysis using the Smith Company (the REIT) Income Statement's for CYE 2006 & 2005:

The Smith Company, Inc.
Comparative Income Statements
CYE

	Horizontal %	Vertical %	2006	Vertical %	2005
Rental Income	114.55%	100.00%	$ 1,059,545	100.00%	$ 925,000
Less: Operating Expenses	111.82%	36.94%	391,361	37.84%	350,000
Operating Income Less:	116.21%	63.06%	668,184	62.16%	$ 575,000
Depreciation Expense Interest	104.18%	12.95%	137,174	14.23%	131,664
Expense	100.60%	38.17%	404,378	43.45%	401,948
Net Income	305.96%	11.95%	$ 126,632	4.47%	$ 41,388

In the above comparative analysis, the vertical common size percentages highlights the decrease in all expenses and corresponding increase in all income figures of CYE 2006 as versus CYE 2005. The horizontal common size analysis shows 2006's rental income increasing at a faster rate than the corresponding 2006 expenses. Horizontal also highlights the small increase in interest expense over 2005 verifying the fact that interest is a fixed expense and consequently does not mimic operating expenses that are more variable.

Ratios are used with the following three strategic comparisons:

1. **TREND ANALYSIS:**

   This is where the company compares its ratios over a period of time of at least two years. Most analysts use 3, 5, or 10 years for their comparisons. The above Smith Company vertical and horizontal analysis is an example of trend analysis for a two year period. Again, three years or more is recommended for this analysis because noticeable trends generally require more than two years to be identified. The information can usually be ascertained from the company's website on the Internet.

2. **COMPETITOR COMPARISONS:**

   This is where you compare the company's ratios with a least one competitor. If you are analyzing Cooper Tire & Rubber, for example, you would use the financial statements of Goodyear or Michelin Tire or both for the comparison. Keep in mind that your company may not be the same size as the main competitor and consequently economies of scale, etc., may distort some ratios for comparitability purposes. The competitor information can also be ascertained directly from their respective websites on the Internet.

3. **INDUSTRY STATISTICS:**

   This is where you compare the company's ratios with other companies within the same industry. These stats can be ascertained from various sources, many of which are Internet. Some websites follow:

   - Yahoo Finance: www.yahoo.com (then select: Finance).

   - Wall Street Journal: www.wsj.com (then select: Money & Investing).

- CBS Market watch: www.marketwatch.com (then select: Comparisons).

- Quicken: www.quicken.com (then select: Company Comparisons).

It should be noted that the statistics for the real estate industry generally includes mostly REIT's and publicly traded real estate partnerships because their information is readily available for compilation. Information for privately held companies, on the other hand, is more difficult to ascertain. Privately held companies are not regulated by the Securities and Exchange Commission and therefore are not required to reveal their financial information to the general public. Directly contacting these companies may be necessary to ascertain their financial statements.

RENTAL REAL ESTATE RATIOS:

The real estate industry has its own specific ratios. The most common and useful ones follow:

INCOME MEASUREMENT RATIOS:

- ### *Efficiency Ratio:*

  Net Rentable Area ∕ Gross Building Area. This ratio is used to determine how much of the total area is being used as net billable space. It is usually calculated using square footage of the area. A higher efficiency ratio is looked at more favorably. Gross Building Area is the premises' entire area. It includes common areas such as walkways, hallways, elevators, etc.

- **Break-even Occupancy Rate:**

  Operating Expenses plus Capital Expenditures plus Debt Service ⁒ Potential Gross Income. This is the percentage of occupancy needed to cover all cash outlays. This rate should be compared to the main competitor and to industry statistics. Higher than break-even occupancy rates are detrimental to the owners and likewise lower than break-even occupancy rates are favorable to the owners. The later would allow increased withdrawals or dividends while the former may require additional owner contributions.

- **Gross Rent Multiplier:**

  Purchase Price of Property ⁒ Potential Gross Income. This ratio gives the multiple of annual rents that a building is being purchased for. It should be compared to like buildings in similar areas. If the ratio is extremely high, it could mean that the purchase price is inflated.

- **Tenant Turnover Rate:**

  Number of New Tenants ⁒ Number of Units. Generally, a low tenant turnover rate means that the tenants are more satisfied with their units. A higher rate would mean the opposite. Again, compare this rate to the main competitor as well as industry statistics.

- **Vacancy Rate:**

  Vacancies ⁒ Potential Gross Income. This ratio indicates how much space is unrented. It should be compared to similar buildings. Keep in mind that macroeconomic events will generally have an effect on this ratio. An example would be that in recessionary periods, this ratio will usually increase.

- *Expense Ratio:*

  Total Operating Expenses ∕. Potential Gross Income. This ratio is used to compare operating expenses with potential gross income. It should be used with trend analysis (should be constant or, better still, decreasing), competitor comparisons (should be hopefully smaller or improved), and industry statistics (should also be smaller or improved). When this ratio rises significantly, great concern should be given to the reasons of why it is rising so rapidly.

- *Income Yield:*

  Net Operating Income ∕. Property Cost. This ratio shows the investor what percentage his or her investment earned for the period. The numerator shows the income currently available for payment of debt service (both mortgage principal and interest) and does not include depreciation expense. Some real estate analysts refer to this ratio as the "Rate of Return on Investment" the "Free & Clear Return" or the "Return on Assets".

- *Cash on Cash Return:*

  After Tax Cash Flow ∕. Initial Equity Investment. Partners and sole proprietors use this ratio. It shows how much their investment earned for them "cash wise" currently net of their tax benefits or expenses. The After tax Cash Flow is Net Operating Income less Debt Service plus Tax savings or less Additional Taxes, whichever pertains. The Tax Savings are allowable losses that are deducted by the owner on their individual income tax returns. It usually means that Interest & Depreciation Expenses are greater than the Net Operating Income. If there were, on the other hand, Additional Taxes, that would mean that the Net Operating Income was greater than the Interest & Depreciation Expenses.

- *Margin of Safety:*

  Cash Available for Debt Service - Debt Service. This positive amount is the cushion that a company has in excess of its current Debt Service liability. Therefore, it should always be a positive figure. Cash Available for Debt Service is Net Operating Income less Capital Expenditures. Debt Service includes both current Principal and Interest Payments. Lenders place great importance to this amount.

- *Debt Service Coverage:*

  Cash Available for Debt Service ∕ Debt Service. This is similar to the Margin of Safety but gives a ratio instead of a dollar figure. It should always be greater than 1. For example, if it is 1.50 times that would mean that the cash available for debt service is 150% of the amount needed to cover the year's current mortgage payments.

- *Times Interest Earned:*

  Net Operating Income ∕ Interest Expense. This ratio records the number of times interest expense could be paid by net operating income. It is used by lenders to show how well their investment is protected. The higher the ratio, the greater the protection. Lenders, incidentally, will be more interested in the Margin of Safety, Debt Service Coverage and appraisal of the mortgaged property as opposed to this ratio.

VALUATION RATIOS:

- *Loan to Value:*

  Mortgage Loan ÷ Property Cost. This ratio shows how much leveraging is involved with the property. The higher the ratio the more leveraged the property. When this ratio grows exceptionally high, lenders may be unwilling to outlay new funds to the company.

- *Debt Ratio:*

  Total Liabilities ÷ Total Assets. This ratio is similar to the Loan to Value ratio but includes all assets and liabilities. Sometimes analysts will also use the market value of the assets when calculating this ratio. This is because in most real estate ventures the lion's share of the assets are realty and because, if anything, the values of the property grow over time.

Chapter
Eight

Utilizing Models for
Decision Making

Utilizing Models for
Decision Making

B usinesses, including real estate entities, use models as tools that help facilitate business decisions. The following is an example of such a model:

REAL ESTATE MODEL FOR DECISION MAKING

You have received a setup (synopsis) of an offering for a 195,000 square foot, 100% leased warehouse building in San Francisco, CA. The set-up shows the following:

Purchase Price:	$24,000,000.00		
Terms:	$4,000,000. cash, balance financed at 8 3/4% with a 25-year level payment, monthly amortization mortgage. (Only 11 payments in 1st year.)		
Commission:	6% to be paid by the seller.		
NOI for 2000:	Rentals & Overages, Net of Vacancies & Debts	$	2,743,000
	Less: Operating Expenses		(893,000)
	Net Operating Income (NOI)	$	1,850,000

ASSUMPTIONS:

Purchase Date:	December 31, 2000.
Rents:	Increase annually @ 5%.
Escalations:	Real Estate Taxes: Increase 2000 Base of $137,150 by 3% per year.
	Labor Cost: Increase 2000 Base of $327,788 by 4% per year.
Operating Expenses:	Increase annually @ 4%.
Depreciable Basis:	80% of the Purchase Price.
Sales Date:	December 31, 2005 (Sales Proceeds are received 12/31/05 also).
Sales Cap Rate:	9 ½ % (Using 2006 NOI).
Selling Costs:	8% of Selling Price (Includes Commissions).
Tax Rate:	39.60%
Capital Gains Tax Rate:	20.00%
Recapture Tax Rate:	25.00%

The following is a model containing questions and answers pertaining to the above offering:

San Francisco California Leased Warehouse Building

QUESTIONS:

	ANSWERS:
a.) What is the net selling price in 2005 (using the year 2006's NOI)?	24,856,216
b.) What was the Before-Tax Cash Flow (BTC) in 2005?	6,682,241
c.) What was the After-Tax Cash Flow (ATC) in 2005?	5,778,493
d.) What was the Margin of Safety in 2001? (Deficit Margin of Safety)	159,940
e.) What was the Cash on Cash Return in 2001? (After-Tax)	5.19%
f.) What is the Net After-Tax Sales Proceeds?	5,434,419
g.) What is the Pre-Tax IRR for the investment?	14.21%
h.) What is the After-Tax IRR for the investment?	11.52%

ASSUMPTIONS:

Purchase Price			24,000,000
Total Square Footage			195,000
Net Annual Rent for 2000			2,743,000
Projected Annual Rental Rate Increase			5.00%
Real Estate Taxes for 2001	Escalation:	3%	137,150
Labor Costs for 2001	Escalation:	4%	327,788
Operating Expenses for 2001 (including Real Estate Taxes & Labor)			893,000
Projected Annual Expense Increase			4.00%
Depreciable Basis			19,200,000
Depreciation Rate			492,308
Sale Cap Rate			9.50%
Sales Commission			6.00%
Selling Costs (Including Sales Commissions)			8.00%
Tax Rate			39.60%
Capital Gains Tax Rate			20.00%
Recapture Tax			25.00%

SALE CALCULATIONS:

Gross Sales Price	27,017,626
Less: Selling Cost (Including Commissions)	2,161,410
Net Sales Price	24,856,216
Less: Adjusted Basis (Net of Accumulated Depreciation)	21,538,462
Taxable Gain on Sale of Building	3,317,754
Less: Recapture Tax	615,385
Capital Gains Tax	171,243
Net Gain on Sale of Building (After Taxes)	2,531,127

ANNUAL DEBT SERVICE:

Purchase Price	24,000,000
Less: Equity Investment	4,000,000
Loan amount	20,000,000
Loan Interest Rate	8.75%
Loan Amortization (Self-Amortizing)	25 Year
Annual Debt Service	(1,973,145)

MORTGAGE AMORTIZATION SCHEDULE: ***

Year	Debt Service	Interest Payments	Principal Payments	Principal Balance
				20,000,000
1	(1,808,716)	1,596,544	212,172	19,787,828
2	(1,973,145)	1,721,501	251,644	19,536,184
3	(1,973,145)	1,698,578	274,567	19,261,617
4	(1,973,145)	1,673,567	299,578	18,962,039
5	(1,973,145)	1,646,275	326,870	18,635,169

*** Only 11 payments in 1st year.

San Francisco California Leased Warehouse Building

			2,000	2,001	2,002	2,003	2,004	2,005	2,006
CASH FLOW PROJECTIONS:			2,000	2,001	2,002	2,003	2,004	2,005	2,006
NET OPERATIONAL CASH FLOW:									
Rentals & Overages, Net of Vacancies & Bad Debts			2,743,000	2,880,150	3,024,158	3,175,365	3,334,134	3,500,840	3,675,882
Add: Escalations									
Real Estate Tax Recovery (3%)			NA	4,115	4,238	4,365	4,496	4,631	4,770
Labor Expense Recovery (4%)			NA	13,112	13,636	14,181	14,749	15,339	15,952
Gross Income			2,743,000	2,897,376	3,042,031	3,193,912	3,353,378	3,520,810	3,696,604
Less: Operating Expenses			893,000	928,720	965,869	1,004,504	1,044,684	1,086,471	1,129,930
Net Operating Income NOI			1,850,000	1,968,656	2,076,163	2,189,408	2,308,695	2,434,339	2,566,674
Less: Replacements									
Cash Available for Debt Service				1,968,656	2,076,163	2,189,408	2,308,695	2,434,339	
Less: Debt Service				(1,808,716)	(1,973,145)	(1,973,145)	(1,973,145)	(1,973,145)	
Gross Operational Cash Flow (Margin of Safety)				159,940	103,018	216,264	335,550	461,194	
Add: Tax Savings (due to pass through losses)				47,597	54,508	585	-	-	
				207,537	157,526	216,849	335,550	461,194	
Less: Tax Expense (due to pass through income)							(56,557)	(117,119)	
Net Operational Cash Flow				207,537	157,526	216,849	278,993	344,075	
OWNERS TAXABLE INCOME OR LOSS:									
Net Operating Income NOI				1,968,656	2,076,163	2,189,408	2,308,695	2,434,339	
Less: Interest Expense				1,596,544	1,721,501	1,698,578	1,673,567	1,646,275	
Less: Depreciation Expense	Total	2,461,538		492,308	492,308	492,308	492,308	492,308	
Taxable Income (Loss)				(120,196)	(137,646)	(1,477)	142,820	295,756	
OWNERS BEFORE & AFTER TAX CASH FLOW									
Purchase/Sales Proceeds (Net)			(4,000,000)					6,221,046	
Operational Cash Flow				159,940	103,018	216,264	335,550	461,194	
Owners Pre-Tax Net Cash Flow			(4,000,000)	159,940	103,018	216,264	335,550	6,682,241	
Add: Tax Savings - Less: Tax Expense				47,597	54,508	585	(56,557)	(117,119)	
Less: Tax on Sale of Building								(786,628)	
Owners After-Tax Net Cash Flow			(4,000,000)	207,537	157,526	216,849	278,993	5,778,493	
Pre-Tax IRR	14.21%								
After-Tax IRR	11.52%								

	A	B	C	D	E	F
1	**San Francisco California Leased Warehouse Building**					
2						
3	QUESTIONS:				ANSWERS:	
4	a.) What is the net selling price in 2005 (using the year 2006's NOI)?				=E34	
5	b.) What was the Before-Tax Cash Flow (BTC) in 2005?				=Sheet2!J32	
6	c.) What was the After-Tax Cash Flow (ATC) in 2005?				=Sheet2!J35	
7	d.) What was the Margin of Safety in 2001? (Deficit Margin of Safety)				=Sheet2!F16	
8	e.) What was the Cash on Cash Return in 2001? (After-Tax)				=SUM(Sheet2!F35/K15)	
9	f.) What is the Net After-Tax Sales Proceeds?				=SUM(E34-#REF!-E37-E38)	
10	g.) What is the Pre-Tax IRR for the investment?				=SUM(Sheet2!D37)	
11	h.) What is the After-Tax IRR for the investment?				=SUM(Sheet2!D38)	
12						
13	ASSUMPTIONS:					
14	Purchase Price				24000000	
15	Total Square Footage				195000	
16	Net Annual Rent for 2000				2743000	
17	Projected Annual Rental Rate Increase				0.05	
18	Real Estate Taxes for 2001		Escalation:	0.03	137150	
19	Labor Costs for 2001		Escalation:	0.04	327788	
20	Operating Expenses for 2001 (including Real Estate Taxes & Labor)				893000	
21	Projected Annual Expense Increase				0.04	
22	Depreciable Basis				=E14*0.8	
23	Depreciation Rate				=1920000/39	
24	Sale Cap Rate				0.095	
25	Sales Commission				0.06	
26	Selling Costs (Including Sales Commissions)				0.08	
27	Tax Rate				0.396	
28	Capital Gains Tax Rate				0.2	
29	Recapture Tax				0.25	
30						
31	SALE CALCULATIONS:					
32	Gross Sales Price				=Sheet2!K12/E24	
33	Less: Selling Cost (Including Commissions)				=E32*E26	
34	Net Sales Price				=SUM(E32-E33)	
35	Less: Adjusted Basis (Net of Accumulated Depreciation)				=SUM(E14-Sheet2!D25)	
36	Taxable Gain on Sale of Building				=SUM(E34-E35)	
37	Less: Recapture Tax				=SUM(E29*Sheet2!D25)	
38	Capital Gains Tax				=SUM(E36-Sheet2!D25)*Sheet1!E28	
39	Net Gain on Sale of Building (After Taxes)				=SUM(E36-E37-E38)	
40						

	G	H	I	J	K	L
1				SHEET 1 OF 2		
2						
3						
4						
5						
6						
7						
8						
9						
10						
11						
12						
13	ANNUAL DEBT SERVICE:					
14	Purchase Price				=E14	
15	Less: Equity Investment				4000000	
16	Loan amount				=SUM(K14-K15)	
17	Loan Interest Rate				0.0875	
18	Loan Amortization (Self-Amortizing)				25 Year	
19	Annual Debt Service				=PMT(8.75%/12.25*12,200000	
20						
21						
22	MORTGAGE AMORTIZATION SCHEDULE: *					
23	Year	Debt	Interest	Principal	Principal	
24		Service	Payments	Payments	Balance	
25					20000000	
26	1	-1808716.25	1596544	212172	19787827.6	
27	2	=Sheet1!K19	1721501	251644	19536184.13	
28	3	=Sheet1!K19	1698578	274567	19261617.28	
29	4	=Sheet1!K19	1673567	299578	18962038.53	
30	*** Only 11 payments in 1st year.					
31						
32						
33						
34						

	A	C	D	E — 2000	F — 2001	G — 2002
1	San Francisco California Leased Warehouse Buildi					
2						
3	CASH FLOW PROJECTIONS:			2000	2001	2002
4						
5	NET OPERATIONAL CASH FLOW:					
6	Rentals & Overages, Net of Vacancies & Bad Debts			=Sheet1!E17	=E6*(1+Sheet1!E18	=F6*(1+Sheet1!E18)
7	Add: Escalations:					
8	Real Estate Tax Recovery (3%)			N/A	=SUM(Sheet1!E19*	=SUM(F8*1.03)
9	Labor Expense Recovery (4%)			N/A	=SUM(Sheet1!E20*	=SUM(F9*1.04)
10	Gross Income			=SUM(E6:E9)	=SUM(F6:F9)	=SUM(G6:G9)
11	Less: Operating Expenses			=Sheet1!E21	=E11*(1+Sheet1!E2	=F11*(1+Sheet1!E22)
12	Net Operating Income NOI			=SUM(E10-E11)	=SUM(F10-F11)	=SUM(G10-G11)
13	Less: Replacements				0	0
14	Cash Available for Debt Service				=SUM(F12-F13)	=SUM(G12-G13)
15	Less: Debt Service				=Sheet1!H27	=Sheet1!K20
16	Gross Operational Cash Flow (Margin of Safety)				=SUM(F14+F15)	=SUM(G14+G15)
17	Add: Tax Savings (due to pass through losses)				=-F26*Sheet1!E28	=-G26*Sheet1!E28
18					=SUM(F16+F17)	=SUM(G16+G17)
19	Less: Tax Expense (due to pass through income)				0	0
20	Net Operational Cash Flow				=SUM(F18-F19)	=SUM(G18-G19)
21						
22	OWNERS TAXABLE INCOME OR LOSS:					
23	Net Operating Income NOI				=F12	=G12
24	Less: Interest Expense				=Sheet1!I27	=Sheet1!I28
25	Less: Depreciation Expense				=Sheet1!E24	=Sheet1!E24
26	Taxable Income (Loss)	Total	=SUM(F25+G25+H		=SUM(F23-F24-F25	=SUM(G23-G24-G25)
27						
28						
29	OWNERS BEFORE & AFTER TAX CASH FLOW					
30	Purchase/Sales Proceeds (Net)			=-Sheet1!K16		
31	Operational Cash Flow				=F16	=G16
32	Owners Pre-Tax Net Cash Flow			=SUM(E30+E31)	=SUM(F30+F31)	=SUM(G30+G31)
33	Add: Tax Savings - Less: Tax Expense			0	=F17	=G17
34	Less: Tax on Sale of Building			0	0	0
35	Owners After-Tax Net Cash Flow			=SUM(E32+E33+E3	=SUM(F32+F33+F3	=SUM(G32+G33+G34)
36						
37	Pre-Tax IRR	=IRR(E32:J32)				
38	After-Tax IRR	=IRR(E35:J35)				
39						

2003	2004	2005	2006
=G6*(1+Sheet1!E18)	=H6*(1+Sheet1!E18)	=SUM(I6*1.05)	=J6*(1+Sheet1!E18)
=SUM(G8*1.03)	=SUM(H8*1.03)	=SUM(I8*1.03)	=SUM(J8*1.03)
=SUM(G9*1.04)	=SUM(H9*1.04)	=SUM(I9*1.04)	=SUM(J9*1.04)
=SUM(H6:H9)	=SUM(I6:I9)	=SUM(J6:J9)	=SUM(K6:K9)
=G11*(1+Sheet1!E22)	=H11*(1+Sheet1!E22)	=I11*(1+Sheet1!E22)	=J11*(1+Sheet1!E22)
=SUM(H10-H11)	=SUM(I10-I11)	=SUM(J10-J11)	=SUM(K10-K11)
0	0	0	
=SUM(H12-H13)	=SUM(I12-I13)	=SUM(J12-J13)	
=Sheet1!K20	=Sheet1!K20	=Sheet1!K20	
=SUM(H14+H15)	=SUM(I14+I15)	=SUM(J14+J15)	
0	0	0	
=-H26*Sheet1!E28	=-I26*Sheet1!E28	=-J26*Sheet1!E28	
=SUM(H16+H17)	=SUM(I16+I17)	=SUM(J16+J17)	
=SUM(H18-H19)	=SUM(I18-I19)	=SUM(J18-J19)	
=H12	=I12	=J12	
=Sheet1!I29	=Sheet1!I30	=Sheet1!I31	
=Sheet1!E24	=Sheet1!E24	=Sheet1!E24	
=SUM(H23-H24-H25)	=I23-I24-I25	=SUM(J23-J24-J25)	
		=Sheet1!E36-Sheet1!K	
=H16	=I16	=J16	
=SUM(H30+H31)	=SUM(I30+I31)	=SUM(J30+J31)	
=H17	=I19	=J19	
0	0	=-(Sheet1!E39+Sheet1	
=SUM(H32+H33+H34)	=SUM(I32+I33+I34)	=SUM(J32+J33+J34)	

Chapter
Nine

Long-term Construction
Contracts

Long-term Construction Contracts

There are two methods for recognizing income for long-term construction projects: The Completed-Contract Method and The Percentage-of-Completion Method. Both these methods are considered specialized accounting methods and are described in the American Institute of Certified Public Accountants (AICPA) Industry Audit and Accounting Guide titled: Construction Contractors. They also are part of the AICPA Statement of Position 81-1 titled: Accounting for Performance of Construction-Type and Certain Production-Type Contracts.

The Completed-Contracted Method generally recognizes income at the end of the contract. This method is _only_ recommended when estimates are unreliable, which should be rarely. When this method is utilized, current costs are accumulated on the balance sheet in a "construction in progress" asset account until the project is completed. Current billings are charged to a "construction in progress" liability account until the project is completed. If a loss can be estimated at any point during the construction, the company will record the estimated loss and reduce this "construction in progress" account for that amount.

The Percentage-of-Completion Method, on the other hand, recognizes income ratably over the life of the contract as it is earned. That's why the Percentage-of-Completion Method is the one most frequently recommended by the AICPA. It mimics the Realization and Matching Concepts of GAAP to a much greater degree than the Completed-Contract Method. As prescribed in Accounting Research Bulletin # 45 (ARB #45) an enterprise is required to disclose which method it uses in accounting for long-term construction contracts.

Chapter
Ten

Synthetic Leases

Synthetic Leases

Note: The FASB or some other regulatory body may disallow Synthetic Leases in the future. The following pertains to Synthetic Leases in general:

Synthetic Leases were originally designed for equipment purchases but are also ideal for real estate construction funding. If it qualifies, the purchaser (lessee/borrower) recognizes the transaction as an operating lease on its financial statements and as an owner on its income tax returns. In other words, the balance sheet does not reflect the asset or the obligation. The income statement reflects only the lease payment expense for the period. The only mention of the liability will be in the notes to the financial statements. This is a type of "off balance sheet financing".

It qualifies as an operating lease if it complies with the Financial Accounting Standards Board Statement Number 13 (SFAS# 13). This statement establishes four criteria for determining whether a lease is a capital lease or operating lease. If any one of the four criteria is met, the lease must be classified as a capital lease with the asset and corresponding mortgage liability being reflected on the balance sheet and depreciation and interest expense being reflected on the income statement. If none of the four criteria pertain, the lease is considered an operating lease. The four criteria are as follows:

1. The lease automatically transfers ownership of the property to the lessee by the end of the lease term.

2. The lease contains a bargain purchase option (this is extremely subjective; must be a significant bargain purchase.)

3. The lease term is equal to 75% or more of the estimated life of the leased property.

4. The present value of the minimum lease payments, at the beginning of the lease term, equals or exceeds 90% of the fair market value of the property, reduced by any Investment Tax Credit retained and expected to be realized by the lessor (prior to determining the 90% base).

It should be noted that the actual cash flow of the lease is not affected by whether it is treated as a capital or an operating lease, but, rather, only how it appears on the lessee's financial statements. In other words, from a lessee's point of view, total cash outlays are the same, but from a leveraging stance, the balance sheet will look more favorable if the transaction qualifies as an operating (synthetic) lease as opposed to a capital lease. This also improves the returns on assets and investment. Synthetic Leases also provide 100% financing.

Finally, it should be noted that the lease has to comply with SFAS #98 or it will be treated as a Sale/Leaseback and lose its operating lease status. In order to retain synthetic lease/operating lease treatment, the lessee cannot have any "continuing involvement" in the property other than as in a "normal" lease. The lessee cannot:

1. Enter into an option to repurchase the property.

2. Guarantee the lessor's investment.

3. Share the appreciation of the property with the lessor.

CPSIA information can be obtained at www.ICGtesting.com
Printed in the USA
BVOW022211091212

307341BV00060B/912/P